ISBN: 9798379216139

Imprint: Independently published

Disclaimer: All answers are correct as of 11th October 2021.

Stenlake Publications presents:

Celtic Crossword

Check out our other books:

Liverpool Crossword
Manchester United Crossword
Arsenal Crossword
Manchester City Crossword
Spurs Crossword
Chelsea Crossword
Leeds Crossword
Rangers Crossword
England Crossword
Newcastle United Crossword
Sunderland Crossword
Leicester City Crossword
England Crossword

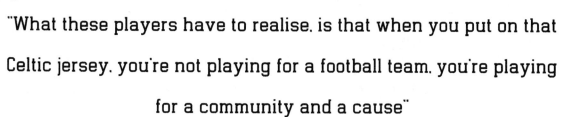

"What these players have to realise. is that when you put on that Celtic jersey. you're not playing for a football team. you're playing for a community and a cause"

- Tommy Burns

"Celtic jerseys are not for second best ... it won't shrink to fit an inferior player"

- Jock Stein

"Best atmosphere I ever played in was at Celtic Park in the UEFA Cup for Liverpool"

- Michael Owen

"I am passionate about football. My support for Celtic FC has got me through como hard times in my life. I still play regularly too"

- Rod Stewart

Contents Page

Round 1 - Founding & History

The Celtic Football Club was founded in 1888 with the purpose of alleviating poverty in the immigrant Irish population in the East End of Glasgow. They won an astonishing 19 league titles pre-WWII and became one of the dominant teams in Scotland. This crossword covers the earliest decades of their history.

Across

4. District of Glasgow that the club was founded in. (6)

10. Celtic's first scorer in their first official match in 1888. (4,8)

12. One-off cup Celtic won in 1945 to celebrate this day – the day of Germany's unconditional surrender to the allies. (7,2,6,3)

13. Glasgow side Celtic encountered while wearing their new hoops design in 1903. (7,7)

16. First manager after becoming a private company in 1897 who went on to spend forty-three consecutive years as manager. (6,5)

17. Celtic's first ever match was against this Glasgow rival. (7)

19. Manager who led Celtic during the World War II years without a single official game. (5,6)

20. Name of the club's founder Brother _____. (7)

Down

1. Now defunct side that beat Celtic in their first Scottish Cup final in 1889. (5,6)

2. Player who scored a hat-trick against Rangers in Scottish Cup final 1904. (5,5)

3. Celtic signed Mohammed Salim in 1936 who was from this Asian nation. (5)

5. The club's official nickname written on the team's postcard back in the early 20th century for their promotion. (3,5,5)

6. All-time record goalscorer with an astonishing 522 goals. (5,7)

7. The first Celtic player called up for the Scotland national team and scored a hat-trick against Ireland at Ibrox. (6,6)

8. Celtic goalkeeper who held the clean sheet record in the UK for 1,287 minutes before the 1920s. (7,4)

9. The old street where Celtic's original ground was located. (10,6)

11. Scotland's oldest club who was Celtic's opponent when they won their first Scottish Cup in 1892. (7,4)

14. Edinburgh side that inspired the club's establishment. (9)

15. Celtic won all four league titles during this war. (5,3,1)

18. Name of the church where the club was officially founded. (2,4)

2

Round 2 - 1950/60s

Celtic struggled for the most part in the 50s and early 60s winning just one league title and one Scottish Cup. That all changed after the arrival of Jock Stein who just two years after his appointment led Celtic to the greatest year in their history winning every trophy available including the 1967 European Cup.

Across

1. Bobby Lennox scored a goal that was disallowed in the 1966 Cup Winners' Cup semi-final at this famous English ground. (7)

4. Opponent Celtic defeated in the 1967 European Cup Final. (5.5)

5. Portuguese side that Celtic beat on a coin toss in the 1970 European Cup quarter-final after blowing a three goal first leg lead. (7)

6. The nickname for Charlie Tully. Celtic's Northern Ireland midfielder in 1950s. (7.4)

8. Gil Heron's country of birth. Celtic's first black player. (7)

9. Soviet team which ended Celtic's Champions Cup campaign as the defending champions. (6.4)

10. The club's official newspaper launched in 1965. (3.6.4)

11. Celtic bought Jock Stein in 1951 as a reserve player from this Welsh league side. (8.4)

13. Celtic won the Coronation Cup in 1953 which celebrated the coronation of this monarch. (9.2)

15. Celtic knocked out Slovan Bratislava in the 1964 Cup Winners' Cup quarter final who are from this modern-day nation. (8)

16. City where they won their first European Cup title in 1967. (6)

17. Celtic lost the Intercontinental Cup against Racing Club who are from this nation. (9)

18. Spanish opposition for Celtic's first match in European competition in the 1962 Inter-Cities Fairs Cup. (8)

Down

2. Side that defeated Celtic in the 1970 European Cup Final. (9)

3. English side that Celtic beat in the 1970 European Cup semi-final. (5.6)

5. Player who netted a hat-trick in their 7-1 win over Glasgow Rangers in 1957/58 Scottish Cup final at Hampden Park. (5.7)

7. French side Celtic knocked out at the early stage in their 1967 Champions Cup campaign. (6)

8. Nicknamed 'Yogi' derived from the popular cartoon character Yogi Bear due to his large build. (4.6)

12. Appointed manager in 1965. (4.5)

14. Celtic faced MTK Budapest in their first European semi-final who are from this country. (7)

The success continued under Stein as they reached another European Cup Final in 1970. won eleven league titles including completing a joint world record nine-in-a-row in 1974. They also won nine Scottish Cups and three League Cups in this 20 -year period.

Across

1. Winger who scored the second goal against Real Madrid in the first leg of the 1981 European Cup quarter-final in European Cup 1981 but tragically died less than a year later. (6,5)

4. Player nicknamed 'Choccy' who spent four seasons at Celtic before 11 seasons at Manchester United where he won four Premier League titles. (5,7)

7. Goalkeeper who saved Atletico Madrid's penalty in the first round of the Cup Winners' Cup in 1986. (3,6)

8. Goalkeeper who made a string of key saves against Real Madrid at the first leg of the quarter finals in the European Cup/Champions League 1980. (5,9)

12. Forward who scored an astonishing 48 goals in all competitions during the 1982/83 season. (7,8)

14. Top scorer in the 1987/88 season with 32 goals in all competitions who had two spells at Celtic either side of three years at Bolton Wanderers. (4,6)

16. Midfielder who went on to play for Dortmund that scored the winning goal against Juventus in the first round of the 1981/82 European Cup. (5,8)

10. Austrian opponents in a brutal 1985 Cup Winners' Cup match. (5,6)

19. Iconic venue for Celtic's last appearance in a European Cup Final. (3,4)

20. Neutral English stadium for the replay of Celtic vs Rapid Vienna after a brutal encounter in Glasgow in the 1985 UEFA Cup Winners' Cup. (3,8)

Down

2. Celtic lost to Sachsenring Zwickau in the 1976 UEFA Winners' Cup who were from this former nation. (4,7)

3. Team who ended Celtic's first "Nine in a row" in 1975. (7)

5. Team which defeated Celtic at the semi-final stage of the 1974 European Cup. (8,6)

6. Portuguese opponent Celtic thrashed 5-0 in the second leg after suffering 0-2 loss at the first leg of UEFA Cup 1984. (8,6)

9. Player who scored in two European Cup finals for Celtic. (5,7)

10. Celtic's only home league defeat of the 1971/72 season came against this Perthshire side. (2,9)

11. Side that defeated Celtic in the 1970 European Cup Final. (9)

13. English team Celtic edged out in the semi-final of the European Cup in 1970. (5,6)

15. Player who scored five goals and was joint top scorer alongside Johan Cruyff in the 1972 European Cup. (3,6)

17. Manager who led Celtic to the 1986 league title. (5,3)

Round 4 - 1990s

The club experienced a slump in the 1990s due to financial difficulties and were saved from the brink of bankruptcy in 1994. During this time arch rivals Rangers dominated Scottish football and matched Celtic's nine-in-a-row before Celtic were able to prevent them beating their record by winning the league in 1998.

Across

1. Scottish international playmaker who moved to Monaco after his six-year spell at Celtic. (4.7)

2. Liverpool and England player who netted an equaliser against Celtic at Parkhead in the UEFA Cup in 1998. (5.9)

10. This kind of animal snuck onto the Celtic Park pitch during a boycotted match against Kilmarnock in 1994. (3)

11. Celtic manager who led the team to the title and prevent Rangers' 10-in-a-row in 1997/98. (3.6)

13. Dutch striker who scored the winning goal in the 1995 Scottish Cup Final. (6.3.9)

15. Slovakian midfielder who scored a brace against Rangers in the famous 5-1 victory in 1998. (4.8)

16. This Australian striker scored the final Celtic goal of the Millenia. (4.6)

18. German side who Celtic came back from a 2-0 first leg deficit to win 3-2 on aggregate in the 1992/93 UEFA Cup. (7)

19. Celtic played their home matches at this stadium for the 1994/95 season whilst Celtic Park was being renovated. (7.4)

Down

1. Defender signed from Dunfermline in 1995 who would go on to make over 350 appearances for the club over 10 seasons. (6.8)

3. Middlesbrough legend who signed for Celtic in 1991 and was later appointed manager in 2009. (4.7)

4. National team of Rudi Vata who played for the club from 1993-96. (7)

5. Nickname given to the 5-1 victory over Rangers in November 1998. "The _____". (7)

6. Striker Dariusz Dziekanowski. who bagged four goals against Partizan Belgrade in the 1990 Cup Winners' Cup is from this nation. (6)

7. Manager who took charge of Celtic for the 1994/95 season. (5.5)

8. Danish midfielder signed from Dundee in 1995 who would go on to make over 100 appearances for the club. (6.9)

9. Manager when Celtic returned to European competition in the 1991/92 season. (4.5)

12. Businessman who saved Celtic from the potential bankruptcy in 1994. (6.6)

14. German international forward signed in 1995. (7.4)

17. Celtic won their first senior trophy since 1989 when they beat this side in the 1995 Scottish Cup Final. (7)

Round 5 - 2000s

A more successful period for the club as they managed to win six out of a possible ten league titles including a treble in 2001. Celtic were pipped to more European glory after losing the 2003 UEFA Cup Final after extra-time. They did however win four Scottish Cups and four League Cups in this decade.

Across

3. Side defeated in the 2003 UEFA Cup semi-finals. (8)

5. Side who Celtic beat on the final day of the 2007/08 season to secure the title. (6.6)

6. Manager guiding The Bhoys to their last European competition final in 2000s. (6.7)

7. Swedish international goalkeeper who was on the Celtic bench for the 2003 UEFA Cup Final. (6.6)

11. Polish goalkeeper who played over 220 games for the club. (5.5)

13. Japanese player who scored a match winning free-kick against Manchester United in 2006. (8.8)

15. Scored a brace for Celtic in the 2003 UEFA Cup Final. (6.7)

16. Highest scoring Welshman in Celtic's history. (4.7)

17. Winger who scored 37 goals in over 250 games between 2003 and 2010. (5.7)

18. Portuguese side which was seeded at the same group with Celtic two seasons in a row in Champions League 2007 and 2008. (7)

19. Manchester United player who failed to convert a penalty against Celtic at Parkhead in a Champions League group stage game in 2007. (5.4)

20. English side that Celtic beat in the 2003 UEFA Cup quarter-final. (9)

Down

1. Irishman signed from Manchester United in 2005. (3.5)

2. Scored the only goal of the tie against Barcelona in the 2003/04 UEFA fourth round. (4.8)

4. Scored a late winning goal against AC Milan in 2007/08 Champions League group stage at Parkhead. (5.8)

8. English forward who holds the record for the quickest goal ever in an Old Firm Clash. scored at Ibrox in 2002. scoring inside just 18 seconds. (5.6)

9. Scored the second goal against Barcelona at the first leg in the round of 16 of Champions League 2008. (5.6)

10. Scored the opening goal in the 2007 victory against AC Milan in the Champions League. (7.7)

12. Porto manager who defeated Celtic in the 2003 UEFA Cup Final. (4.8)

14. New Zealand international signed from Hibs in 2007. (5.6)

Round 6 - 2010s

The 2010s were one of the most successful in the club's history as they dominated Scottish football, partly helped by the demise of Rangers to the fourth tier. They won eight of the ten league titles available, five Scottish Cups and four League Cups including three trebles.

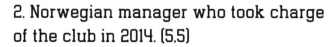

Across

2. Norwegian manager who took charge of the club in 2014. (5.5)

4. Team which Efe Ambrose signed for in 2017 after leaving Celtic. (9)

6. Scored the winner against Barcelona in the 2013 Champions League. (4.4)

10. Russian side that Aiden McGeady was sold to for £9.5m in 2010. (7.6)

12. Player who scored the late winning goal in the 2017 Scottish Cup Final. (3.5)

15. English side that Christian Gamboa was signed from in 2014. (4.8.6)

16. Irish loanee who was top scorer in the 2009/10 season with 18 goals despite only joining in January. (6.5)

17. Swedish right back who represented the club for eight seasons. (6.6)

18. National team of Victor Wanyama. (5)

19. Manager appointed in May 2016. (7.7)

20. English-born Scotland international who scored 91 goals in 227 appearances between 2010 and 2017. (4.7)

Down

1. Celtic sealed the treble treble with victory against this side in the 2019 Scottish Cup Final. (5.2.10)

3. Striker signed from Scunthorpe who'd go on to score 82 goals for the club in four seasons. (4.6)

5. Arsenal and Sweden legend signed on a short-term deal in 2011. (7.9)

7. Scored the opening goal against Aberdeen in the 2017 Scottish Cup Final which helped seal the treble. (6.9)

8. Winger nicknamed "The Derry Pele". (5.7)

9. Player who scored a late equaliser against Inter Milan in the first leg of the Europa League 2015 in the round of 32. (4.8)

11. Player who missed a penalty against Barcelona on the road in the Champions League 2017. (6.7)

13. Striker signed from Manchester City in 2008, initially on loan. (8,7)

14. Club that Fraser Forster was signed from. (9.6)

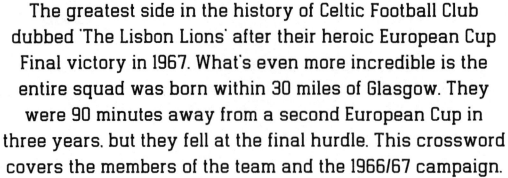

The greatest side in the history of Celtic Football Club dubbed 'The Lisbon Lions' after their heroic European Cup Final victory in 1967. What's even more incredible is the entire squad was born within 30 miles of Glasgow. They were 90 minutes away from a second European Cup in three years. but they fell at the final hurdle. This crossword covers the members of the team and the 1966/67 campaign.

Across

2. The illness Stevie Chalmers suffered in 2017 which prevented him from attending the 50 years anniversary of the Lisbon Lions. (7)

4. Swiss team who Celtic beat in the first round. (6)

5. Right-back whose tackle led to Inter's penalty in the final. (3,5)

7. The team was famous because all of Celtic's players were born within this radius from Glasgow (in miles). (6)

11. Celtic played Dukla Prague in the semi-finals who were from this former nation. (14)

12. Jock Stein's assistant manager in the 1966/67 season. (4,6)

13. Host stadium of the final which translates to English as National Stadium. (7,8)

14. Legendary left-back who was in the starting XI for Inter. (8,9)

15. Started left-wing and wore the number 11 shirt for Celtic. (5,6)

17. Celtic's goalkeeper for the final. (6,7)

18. Number 10 who started in midfield who had two spells with Celtic in between a spell with Birmingham City. (6,3)

19. Midfielder who provided an assist for the second goal in the final. (5,6)

Down

1. Celtic's quarter-final opponents were Vojvodina who came from this former nation at the time. (10)

3. French opponents nicknamed 'Les Canaries' who Celtic beat in the second round. (6)

6. The English team Billy McNeill took charge of from 1983 to 1986. (10,4)

8. Defensive tactical system used by Inter and many other teams of that era. (10)

9. Scored the winning goal in the final. (6,8)

10. Inter Milan player who Jim Craig brought down in the final which led to Nerrazurri's penalty. (6,10)

15. Liverpool manager who said of Jock Stein for his achievement "John. you're immortal now". (4,7)

16. Tommy Gemmell would later win the 1973 Scottish Cup Final against Celtic playing for this team. (6)

14

Round 8 - Jock Stein

The club's greatest manager. Jock Stein won an incredible 10 league titles. 8 Scottish Cups. 6 League Cups and the European Cup among others during his thirteen years as manager as well as a handful of trophies as a player with the club. He was also manager of the Scottish national team and is honoured with a statue outside Celtic Park.

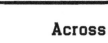

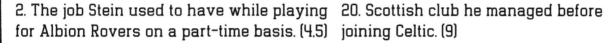

Across

2. The job Stein used to have while playing for Albion Rovers on a part-time basis. (4,5)

4. Scotsman who was Stein's only major signing of the 1965/66 season and would reward him with 43 goals in his debut season. (3,7)

6. The Welsh stadium where he had a heart attack and passed away not long after the match he oversaw. (6,4)

10. Famous Scottish sculptor who created Stein's bronze statue outside Celtic Park. (4,7)

11. His predecessor for the Scotland national team before he was appointed as full-time manager. (4,7)

13. English side who made an offer for their managerial position in the 1964/65 season. (13,9)

14. Stein won nine league titles in a row, a joint-world record with MTK Budapest of Hungary and CSKA Sofia who are from this nation. (8)

17. Stein blamed this defender for not marking Kai Johansen which led to the winning goal in the 1966 Scottish Cup Final. (4,6)

18. English side which Stein signed for before accepting the offer from the Scotland national team. (5,6)

19. Stein's new assistant at Celtic during the 1976/77 season. (5,9)

20. Scottish club he managed before joining Celtic. (9)

Down

1. First team Jock Stein met in the 1982 World Cup while taking charge of the Scotland national team.

3. Stein became the second manager to take charge of (answer to clue 18) for just 44 days after this man. (5,6)

5. Fife-based club which was Steins first managerial job. (11,8)

7. Celtic's branch company which Stein was given an offer for a managerial position at the end of his spell in 1978. (5,7)

8. Appointed interim manager of Scotland after Stein's sudden death in 1985. (4,8)

9. Club legend who Stein nominated to be his successor as manager. (5,7)

12. County that Stein was born in. (11)

15. Player surprisingly signed by Stein from Tottenham Hotspur who became the first player post-WWII player to play for Celtic and Rangers. (5,4)

16. Opposition that Scotland famously beat 3-1 at Hampden in 1984 which Stein described as the most satisfying since I became [Scotland] manager".

Round 9 - Managers

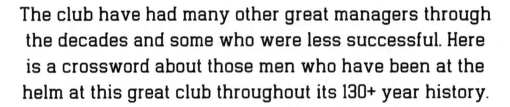

The club have had many other great managers through the decades and some who were less successful. Here is a crossword about those men who have been at the helm at this great club throughout its 130+ year history.

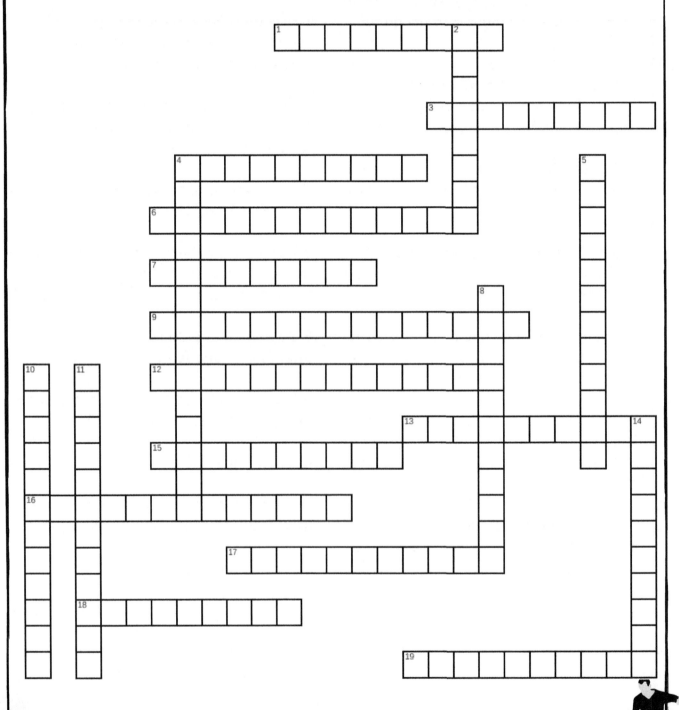

Across

1. First ever Celtic manager who hadn't previously played for the club. (4,5)

3. Dutchman who was Celtic's first non-British or Irish manager. (3,6)

4. Former St. Mirren man who had been a caretaker at Celtic during the 1990s and Scotland national team in the mid 2010s. (5,5)

6. Club that Brendan Rodgers left for in February 2019 despite being eight points clear at the top of the table. (9,4)

7. Former Bournemouth manager who turned down the Celtic job in 2021. (5,4)

9. Manager appointed in June 2021. (4,11)

12. Celtic's only permanent Scottish manager since 1997. (6,8)

13. Non-managerial position that David Hay took up upon returning to the club in the mid-1990s. (5,5)

15. Won five Scottish Premierships as a Celtic player and five as manager. (4,6)

16. Tony Mowbray's next club after he was dismissed from Parkhead. (13)

17. Manager who has managed the most games for Celtic with 1,617. (6,5)

18. Nationality of Rony Deila. (9)

19. Liverpool and England legend who had a brief stint as manager from 1999-2000. (4,6)

Down

2. Took charge for over 200 games after being forced to retire as a player aged 31 due to a detached retina. (5,3)

4. Manager who used to work under Jose Mourinho. (7,7)

5. Led Czechoslovakia to a third-place finish at the 1980 Euros and the 1990 World Cup quarter-final. (5,7)

8. Caretaker manager for 10 games between February and June of 2021. (4,7)

10. Racked up nearly 1,400 games as player and manager for the club. (5,7)

11. One of Tommy Burns' famous signings who once played for Juventus, Napoli and AC Milan. (5,2,5)

14. Made over 500 appearances for the club before three years as manager in the 90s. (5,5)

Round 10 - Jimmy McGory

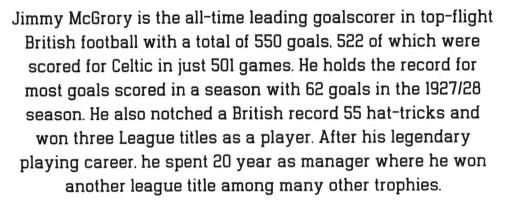

Jimmy McGrory is the all-time leading goalscorer in top-flight British football with a total of 550 goals. 522 of which were scored for Celtic in just 501 games. He holds the record for most goals scored in a season with 62 goals in the 1927/28 season. He also notched a British record 55 hat-tricks and won three League titles as a player. After his legendary playing career. he spent 20 year as manager where he won another league title among many other trophies.

Across

1. Good friend and teammate who tragically died after a game against Rangers in 1931 due to a fractured skull sustained during the match. (4.8)

4. The only scorer in the Scottish Cup Final 1951. which was McGrory's first trophy for the Bhoys. (4.7)

5. London club who was scouting McGrory before he joined Celtic. (6)

12. Celtic's contender in a title race when he clinched his first league title as a manager in 1954. (5.2.10)

14. His parents were immigrants from this traditional Irish province. in the north of Ireland. (6)

15. Team he was sent on loan to in his early years with Celtic. (9)

16. Celtic's second top scorer of all-time who is 201 goals behind McGrory. (5.6)

17. Celtic chairman who made a move to offer him a managerial position at Parkhead. (3.5)

18. Club who he scored the fastest hat-trick in Scottish League history against. doing so within 3 minutes in 1936. (10)

Down

2. McGrory was often overlooked for national team selection in favour of this player. (6.9)

3. Opponent Jimmy McGrory played against in his first and final international game. (7)

4. His predecessor as manager of Celtic. (5.6)

5. The home of Partick Thistle. where he made his international debut in 1928. (6)

6. His first managerial job. (10)

7. His successor as manager at Celtic. (4.5)

8. Manager who signed him for Celtic from junior side St Roch. (6.5)

9. London club that had a world record £10,000 bid accepted by Celtic. but McGrory turned down the move. (7)

10. Jimmy McGrory's nickname for being a prolific goal scorer. (5.7)

11. Old district name in Glasgow where he was born. (7)

13. He created what is still a Celtic. Scottish and British record for the most goals in a top-flight League match by one player. with 8 goals in a 9-0 win over this side in 1928. (11)

Round 11 - Billy McNeill

Billy McNeill's association with Celtic spans over 60 years. He was captain of the Lisbon Lions and holds the record for most appearances with 822 across 18 seasons. He won 31 major trophies as a player and his two spells as manager. He is one of a few men to have a statue outside Celtic Park and is without doubt one of the all-time greats.

Across

4. He scored in a third Scottish Cup Final in 1972 against this opposition. (9)

8. Manager who said "What makes a great player? He's the one who brings out the best in others. When I am saying that I'm talking about Billy McNeill." (4.5)

13. His first managerial job was this North Lanarkshire side. (5)

14. He left Celtic as manager after the board sold this player to Arsenal in 1983 against his wishes. (7.8)

15. His final Celtic game was the 1975 Scottish Cup Final against this opposition. (7)

17. His successor at Aberdeen after he left the post. (4.8)

18. Nation he scored against for Scotland in the 1968/69 Home Championship. (5)

Down

1. McNeill scored in the 1969 Scottish Cup Final against this side. (7)

2. English side who he won promotion to the First Division with as manager. (10.4)

3. Chairman he had a dispute regarding his compensation and transfer policy (7.5)

4. Title of the autobiography he wrote and published in 2004. (4.5)

5. Name of his second autobiography. (4.2.8)

6. County where he was born. (11)

7. Spanish club that gave him the 'One Club Award' in 2019 for his loyalty and contribution to Celtic. (8.9)

8. His player who was sent off in the final match of the 1978/79 season when McNeill clinched his first league title. (6.5)

9. Role he was given by Celtic in 2009. (4.10)

10. One of his signings during his reign at Aberdeen who then played for Barcelona in 1980s. (5.9)

11. English side he was relegated with as manager in his only season as manager. (5.5)

12. His maternal grandparents were from this Baltic nation. (9)

16. Mediterranean island nation he scored his final Scotland goal against. (6)

Round 12 - Celtic Park

Celtic Park on its current site has been Celtic's spiritual home since 1892, four years after the club's inception. It is now the largest stadium in Scotland and eighth largest in the UK and has hosted Scotland internationals and Scottish Cup Finals and seen many great Celtic highs through the decades.

Across

4. Part of the North Grandstand was destroyed by a ____ in 1904. (4)

6. Scotland beat this Baltic side at Celtic Park to secure qualification to the 1998 World Cup. (6)

7. Stadium's facility installed in 1959. (11)

10. Celtic built the first of its kind in a British football stadium in 1894. (5.3)

11. The area which was initially chosen to build Celtic's new home ground before Fergus McCann cancelled it out and opted to renovate Parkhead during the 90s. (10)

15. The opening ceremony of this sporting event was held in 2014 at Celtic Park. (12.5)

17. Scotland played at Celtic Park in a game against the Faroe Islands in 2006 after Hampden was double booked with a concert for this singer and entertainer. (6.8)

18. Alternative nickname of Celtic Park beside 'Parkhead'. (8)

19. Rangers' opponents in the 1993 Scottish Cup Final held at Celtic Park. (0)

20. English opponent that Celtic played against in 1995 to celebrate the reopening of Celtic Park with a new North Stand. (9.6)

Down

1. Name of the Scottish cyclist who the Commonwealth Arena and Velodrome on the site of Celtic Park is named after. (5.3)

2. This report required all stadiums in the UK to become all-seaters. (6)

3. The closest railway station to Celtic Park. (10)

5. The last Scotland international held at Celtic Park was in 2014 against this side. (7)

8. Name of the east stand. (6.5)

9. A statue of this man was erected in 2005 outside the main stand. (7.7)

12. The stand which used to be the site of the West Terracing is named after this man. (4.5)

13. Venue 'The Bhoys' used as their home turf in the 1928/29 season due to the fire at Celtic Park in 1929 which is now used exclusively for greyhound racing. (9.7)

14. Nickname of the northern Hayshed terrace which became well-recognised during the 1960s. (6)

16. East Glasgow district that Celtic Park is located in. (8)

Round 13 - Academy Graduates

The Celtic academy is renowned around the world for producing great talents. Can you name this select group of 20 players based on these clues?

Across

3. Signed a pre-contract agreement with Manchester United in 2004 after Martin O'Neill wanted to build his new Celtic team around him. (4.6)

4. Played in every position except striker and goalkeeper in his 24 appearances with the club before making 159 appearances for Birmingham. mainly at right-back. (4.6)

5. Midfielder who made 37 appearances before leaving in 2018 to forge a career in Italy. (4.9)

7. Part of the 1981/82 title winning team and would go on to manage Everton. Manchester United and West Ham among others. (5.5)

10. Scored 29 goals in 35 games in the 1982/82 season before joining Arsenal. He would score 127 goals across two spells for Celtic. (7.8)

11. Centre-back who has played for clubs in Scotland. England. Canada. Ukraine and India. as well as the Republic of Ireland (6.4)

13. Scored 16 goals in 65 games before being snapped up by West Brom for £1.5 million in 2007. (5.7)

15. Earned a record 102 full caps for the Scotland national team. scoring 30 goals. also a joint-record and won the Ballon d'Or Silver Award in 1983. (5.8)

16. Scottish-born Republic of Ireland international and became the most expensive export from Scottish football after a £9.5 million move in 2010. (5.7)

17. 17. No-nonsense defender who made over 200 appearances for the club and scored in a 2-1 Champions League victory against holders AC Milan in 2007. (7.7)

18. One-club man who has made over 400 appearances for the club and counting and scored a hat-trick against Israel for Scotland in 2018. (5.7)

19. Australian international who made his sole league appearance for the club in 2012. (7.6)

20. Irish midfielder who left without making a league appearance who'd go on to represent St Mirren. Ross County. Plymouth Argyle and CSKA Sofia. (6.5)

Down

1. Scored in two successive Old Firm victories against Rangers in the space of a week in April 2017 and scored for Scotland at Euro 2020. (6.8)

2. Gained widespread media attention after making his debut for Celtic's Under-20 side aged 13 and made his first team debut at the age of 16. (8.7)

6. Scottish international goalkeeper who had a stand-out performance against Barcelona in a 2004 UEFA Cup tie before making over 500 appearances in England. (5.8)

8. Malaysian-born Scottish international winger who won five titles over two spells with the club between 2001 and 2011. (5.7)

9. Free-kick specialist centre-back who won the SPL Players' and writers' player of the year awards for 2011-12. (7.7)

12. Winger who signed a new five-year contract with Celtic on 28 December 2019. (5.9)

14. Isle of Man-born left-back sold for a record Scottish national and Scottish League fee of £25 million. (6.7)

Round 14 - Club Captains

The club have had many legendary captains in their history. Can you name the last 20 based on their years as captain as well as the number of appearances and goals for the club?

Across

3. 1977-87 - 679 apps. 9 goals. (5.7)

6. 1990-97 - 678 apps. 72 goals. (4.6)

8. 2002-04 - 252 apps. 19 goals. (4.7)

9. 1957-61 - 453 apps. 50 goals. (6.7)

10. 1955-57 - 549 apps. 11 goals. (5.5)

11. 1963-75 - 789 apps. 37 goals. (5.7)

12. 2004-05 - 299 apps. 15 goals. (6.8)

15. 1961-63 - 236 apps. 7 goals. (6.6)

16. 1953-55 - 148 apps. 2 goals. (4.5)

18. 2021-present - 334 apps. 54 goals and counting. (6.8)

19. 1948-52 - 335 apps. 100 goals. (4.7)

20. 2005-07 - 300 apps. 3 goals. (4.6)

Down

11. 1975-77 - 322 apps. 167 goals. (5.8)

2. 1935-39 - 163 apps. 0 goals. (6.4)

4. 1987-90 - 667 apps. 55 goals. (3.6)

5. 1934-35 - 575 apps. 0 goals. (5.4)

7. 2007-10 - 200 apps. 20 goals. (7.7)

13. 1952-53 - 254 apps. 14 goals. (4.6)

14. 2010-21 - 619 apps. 46 goals. (5.5)

17. 1997-2002 - 349 apps. 2 goals. (3.4)

Round 15 - Henrik Larsson

The club's greatest ever foreign player, third highest goalscorer and second highest goal scorer in the SPL. Henrik Larsson scored an astonishing 242 goals in 315 matches, winning the League's golden boot in five of the six seasons he played in as well as four league titles, two Scottish Cups, two League Cups, and scored twice in Celtic's first European Final since 1970 in 2003.

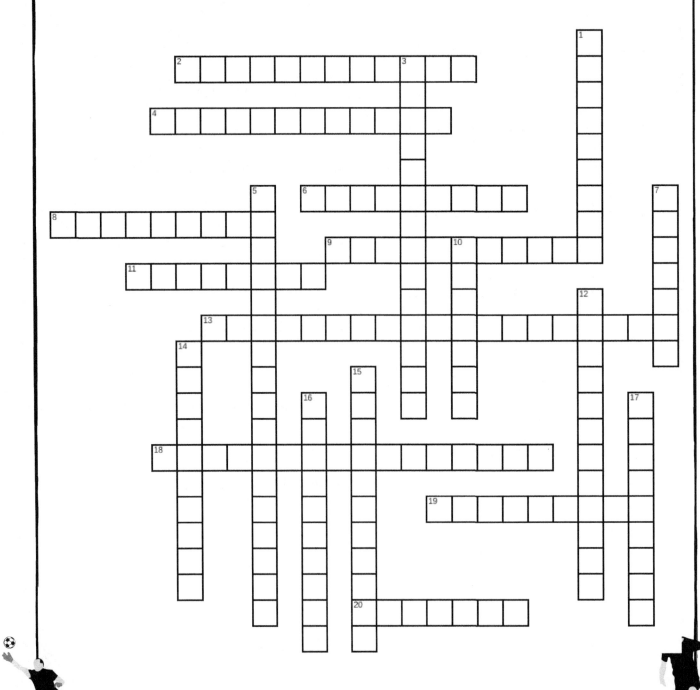

Across

2. He helped Sweden to achieve a national record third place at the 1994 World Cup which was hosted in this country. (6.6)

4. Larsson earnt his first medal with Celtic after a 3-0 win over this team in the 1997 League Cup Final. (6.6)

6. Dutch club that Larsson was signed from by Celtic. (9)

8. The other sport he played professionally. (9)

9. He scored a brace against this side to win Celtic's first league title since 1988 and prevented Rangers breaking Celtic's record of nine titles in a row. (2.9)

11. Larsson scored in Celtic's first ever math in the rebranded Champions League with a goal away at this Italian giant. (8)

13. His last Celtic game was the 2004 Scottish Cup Final against this club. (11.8)

18. English club that he won a Premier League title with during a short loan spell. (10.6)

19. Club that he won the Champions League with. (9)

20. He scored against this nation at the 2006 World Cup. (7)

Down

1. His father's country of origin. (4.5)

3. Nickname given to him by Celtic fans. (3.4.2.5)

5. The only player to win more Guldbollen awards than Larsson. awarded for the best male Swedish player each season. (6.11)

7. The Portuguese club he had a trial at the age of 18. (7)

10. Opponent he bagged a brace against at the 2002 World Cup. (7)

12. Hometown club where he played from 1992-93 and 2006-09 as well as two spells as manager. (12)

14. Rangers' German goalkeeper who was between the posts for the "demolition derby' where Larsson scored a famous chip. (6.4)

15. He achieved a career high 13th in the 2003 Ballon d'Or award which was won by this player. (5.6)

16. Venue where he made his debut for Celtic in 1997. (6.4)

17. Celtic manager who signed him. (3.6)

Round 16 - Neil Lennon

Neil Lennon made 300 appearances as a player for Celtic before taking the reigns as manager over two spells between 2010 and 2021. In all, he won ten league titles, eight Scottish Cups and three League Cups as player and manager across his fourteen-year association with the club. He guided Celtic to five of the nine-in-a-row and also to the Champions League knockout stages. He is without doubt a modern-day club legend.

Across

1. English club he managed after leaving Celtic in 2014. (6.9)

3. His predecessor as manager of Celtic. (4.7)

4. Israeli who sits joint-5th with Lennon on Celtic's all-time record transfer fee paid.

6. Manager who signed him for Celtic from his former club. (6.6)

7. Last opponent in Lennon's second spell before resigning in 2021. (4.6)

8. Championship club he was in charge of after leaving Celtic in 2014. (6.9)

12. English club where Lennon started his professional career. (5.9)

14. Lennon was born in Lurgan which is in this Northern Irish County. (6)

16. Former teammate who became his assistant when Lennon took charge of Celtic in 2010. (5.7)

17. Club that Celtic signed Lennon from in 2000. (9.4)

18. International goalkeeper he sold during the 2010/11 season as a part of revamping the squad. (5.5)

Down

1. Star studded side he masterminded one of Celtic all-time great performances against in 2012. (9)

2. The Scottish club he won promotion with in his first season with before qualifying for Europe in his second. (9)

3. Merseyside opponent he played against in the 2000 League Cup Final victory. (8.6)

5. Central American player who Lennon bought in that would win the Scottish Premier League Player of the Year for the 2010/11 season. (6.9)

9. Lennon was targeted with bigoted abuse by opposition fans and even his own national team as he was a member of this religion. (5.8)

10. Lennon's Celtic famously defeated this side in the 2019/20 Europa League group stage 2-1 in both games. (5)

11. Former Celtic midfielder who was Lennon's boss at Wycombe Wanderers. (4.7)

13. Lennon was criticized for taking his players on a training camp to this Middle East city in January 2021 where two of his players contracted Covid-19. (5)

15. Welsh international player he signed for free in 2010. (3.6)

Two members of the 'Lisbon Lions' and named as the wingers in Celtic's greatest ever team voted for by fans in 2002. They racked up 436 goals in 1,086 appearances in the 60s and 70s. They are two of the greatest players that Scotland have ever produced and won every trophy possible for the club.

Across

3. Johnstone's best friend who was a former Rangers player and the last one to call him before his death. (6.9)

5. Documentary film about Johnstone's life broadcast on the BBC in 2004. (4.2.3.4)

6. Lennox's final Celtic game was the 1980 Scottish Cup Final against this side. (7)

10. Legendary Celtic left-back who signed as a youth player on the same day as Johnstone. (5.7)

11. Phobia that Jimmy Johnstone had. (6)

12. Yugoslavian team that Jimmy scored two goals and provided three assists against in the 1968/69 European Cup. (3.4.8)

13. Johnstone finished third in the 1967 Ballon d'Or. one point ahead of this German great. (5.11)

15. Johnstone scored his sole World Cup qualifying goal for Scotland away in West Germany at the Volksparkstadion in this city. (7)

17. The only other club Lennox played for was the Houston Hurricane who are from this US state. (5)

18. Lennox placed third in the 1967/68 European Golden Boot which was won by this Benfica and Portugal legend. (7)

19. County that Bobby Lennox was born in. (8)

20. One of Lennox's nicknames. (4.4)

Down

1. Legendary Argentinian and Real Madrid player who admired Lennox greatly despite being less well-known than Jimmy Johnstone after his testimonial match. (7.2.7)

2. Type of fruit that is one of Lennox's nicknames after a spelling mistake by a journalist. (5)

4. Johnstone's nickname. (5)

7. Yorkshire side that Johnstone played for after a spell in the USA. (9.6)

8. Johnstone scored twice against this Dutch side en route to the 1965 Cup Winners' Cup semi-finals. (3.5.6)

9. Manager who re-signed Lennox for Celtic in 1979. (5.7)

14. Manchester United and England legend who said "If I'd had Lennox in my team. I could have played forever. He was one of the best strikers I have ever seen" (5,8)

16. Lennox became the first Celtic player to score at this iconic international stadium in 1967. (7)

Round 18 - General I

You've done well to reach this point: I hope you have learned lots of cool facts about the Bhoys. Here are three rounds of general questions from a range of categories to finish off. Good luck!

Across

3. Australian forward who spent two years at Parkhead before thriving at Leeds United and Middlesbrough. (4.6)

5. Scottish international who moved from Chelsea to Parkhead in 1997 and scored at the 1998 World Cup. (5.6)

7. Joe Hart's shirt number when he opted to join Celtic in 2021. (7)

9. Italian midfielder who was loaned out five times as an AC Milan player before completing his move to Celtic in 2007. (7.6)

10. Australian side that Tom Rogic was signed from. (7.5.8)

13. Club that Paul Lambert won the Champions League with before moving to Parkhead. (8.8)

16. Midfielder who won ten trophies with Celtic but suffered from leukaemia towards the end of his playing career. (8.6)

17. John Collins scored his only World Cup goal in 1998 against this nation. (5)

18. Kit manufacturer from 1960s to 2005. (5)

19. French wing-back who made 122 appearances for The Bhoys in six years including the 2003 UEFA Cup final. (6.6)

Down

1. Czech midfielder who joined Celtic after only playing less than 20 games under Jose Mourinho in Chelsea. (4.7)

2. Russian goalkeeper who joined under John Barnes but only made 11 appearances despite his appearances at Euro '92 and World Cup '94. (6.7)

4. Talented attacking midfielder who became a legend at Middlesbrough before moving to Parkhead in 2004. (7.8)

5. Player who netted the winner against Lazio in the home game at the group stage of the Europa League in 2020. (11.7)

6. Israel international who signed for Brighton after his five-year stint at Celtic. (5.5)

8. Number of goals Kris Commons scored when he was top scorer in the 2013/14 Scottish Premiership. (6.5)

11. Celtic spent the largest transfer fee between two Scottish clubs to capture this player. (5.5)

12. Irish cider brand that sponsored the club from 2013-16. (7)

14. English striker who is the oldest debutant in Celtic's history when he was already 36 years old in 2006. (4.5)

15. Striker who holds the joint Scottish Premier League record for goals in a game with five against Hearts in 2012. (4.6)

Across

1. Barcelona player who had a penalty saved by David Marshall in a 2004/05 Champions League game at Parkhead. (10)

4. Celtic and Rangers joined forces to seal this terminology of their exclusive rivalry at the Intellectual Property Office in 2000. (3.4)

5. Versatile attacking midfielder who had two spells in Celtic and was born in Malaysia. (5.7)

6. Dutch centre-back who scored after a long solo run in a game against St Johnstone in 2013. (6.3.4)

8. Surname of Patrik and Filip. the Czech twins who joined Celtic's youth team in 2009 but failed to thrive in the first team after staying for several years. (8)

9. Italian club which Celtic signed Shunsuke Nakamura from. (7)

12. The youngest player to play in European competition for the club. (8.7)

14. Famous Celtic fan who starred in the movies Split. Filth and The Last King of Scotland among others. (5.6)

16. Danish midfielder who spent most of his time at Parkhead being sidelined due to his injuries but managed to play three games at the 1998 World Cup. (6.9)

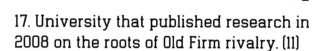

17. University that published research in 2008 on the roots of Old Firm rivalry. (11)

18. Talented attacking midfielder and Middlesbrough legend who moved to Parkhead in 2004. (7.8)

19. Defender who spent the 2014/15 season on loan from Manchester City. (5.7)

Down

2. Nigerian Efe Ambrose was signed from S.C Ironi Ashdod in 2012 who are from this nation. (6)

3. Goalkeeper who started the 2003 UEFA Cup Final. (3.7)

5. Midfielder who won ten trophies with Celtic but suffered leukaemia towards the end of his playing career. (8.6)

7. Side that Celtic beat on the 17th of April 1948 to avoid relegation. (6)

10. Club that Roy Keane scored his only goal for The Bhoys in his brief stint. (7)

11. Striker who played for both Celtic and Rangers after the millennium. (5.6)

13. Actress known for her roles in Doctor Who. Jumanji and several Marvel films who is a Celtic fan. (5.6)

15. Holds the record for most European appearances with 127. (5.5)

Across

3. Celtic have gone through a penalty shootout three times in European competition. The third one was against this Russian side. (7.6)

4. Shirt sponsor from 1999-2003. (3)

5. Celtic striker who netted a brace in 2017 for the Tartan Army against England in a World Cup 2018 qualifier. (5.9)

10. Dutch defender who became the target of Rangers and Celtic before eventually signing for the Bhoys in 2008. (5.7)

12. The first Norwegian player ever to play for Celtic who scored all four goals on the final day of the 1997/98 season to secure the title. (6.9)

14. The first foreign-born Korean player to play in a World Cup who played for Celtic between 2010 and 2012. (3.2.2)

17. Former East Germany player who signed from Bayer Leverkusen in 1995 for a then club record fee of £2.2m. (7.4)

18. Barcelona academy product who spent three seasons at Parkhead before moving to Russia in 2011. (4.6)

19. Shaun Maloney's shirt number for the 2010/11 season. (8)

20. Jan Vennegoor of Hesselink's next club after leaving Celtic Park in 2009. (4.4)

Down

1. South Korean midfielder who made 87 appearances for the club between 2009 and 2012. (2.4.5)

2. Versatile defensive player who earned 33 caps for Scotland and made more than 250 appearances for Celtic before becoming a manager. (6.8)

6. Club that John Hartson was signed from in 2001. (8.4)

7. A group of fanatic Celtic supporters formed in 2006 who are normally seated on the North Curve of Celtic Park. (5.7)

8. Celtic player voted as the SFWA Footballer of the Year in 2015. (5.6)

9. Fraser Forster's back-up at Celtic during the 2010/11 season who helped the team break the previous clean sheet record from the 2001/02 season. (6.7)

11. Nation that Aiden McGeady was born in. (8)

13. Player nicknamed 'The Maestro' who has won the most international caps whilst being a Celtic player with 76. (4.6)

15. Shirt sponsor from 2003 to 2010. (7)

16. National team of Bobo Baldé. (6)

Answers

Round 1 - Founding & History

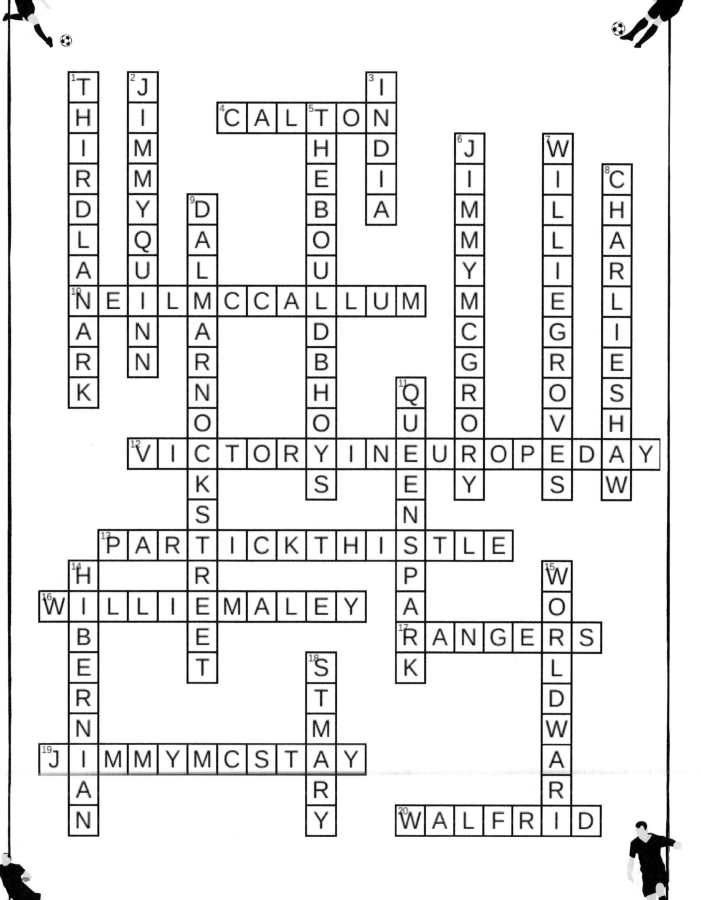

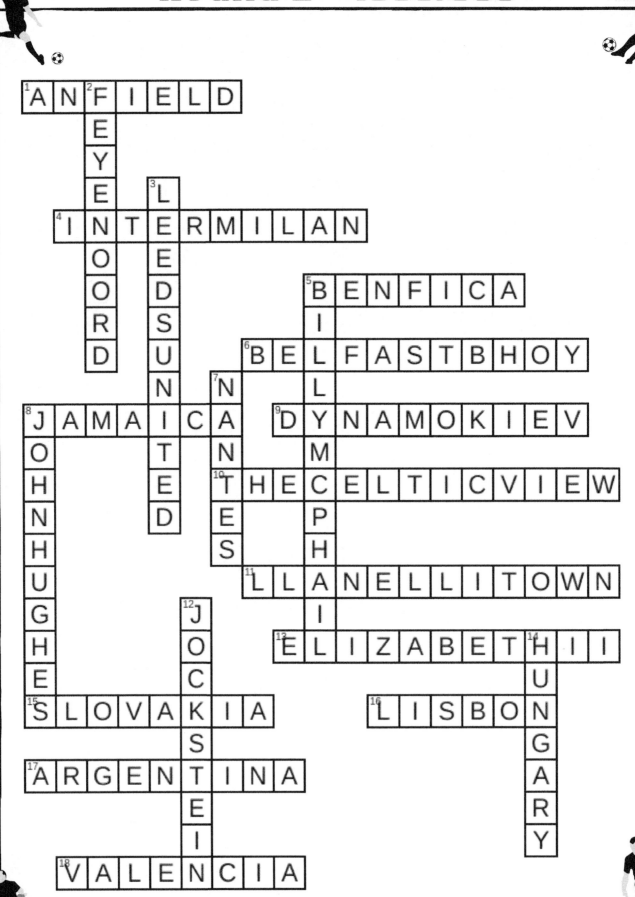

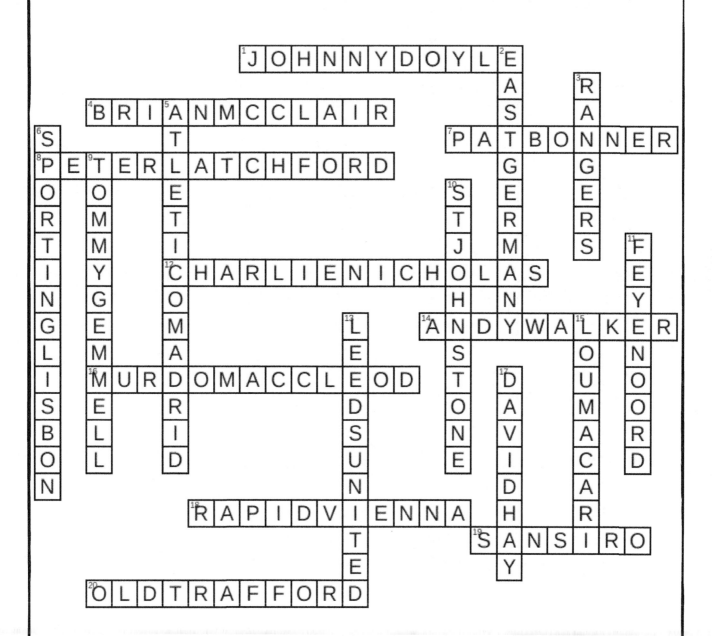

The crossword grid contains the following answers:

1. JOHNNYDOYLE
2. EASTGERMANS
3. RANGERS
4. BRIANMCCLAIR
5. ATLETICOMADRID
6. SPORTINGLISBON
7. PATBONNER
8. PETERLATCHFORD
9. TOMMYGEMMELL
10. STJOHNSTONE
11. FEYENOORD
12. CHARLIENICHOLAS
13. LEEDSUNITED
14. ANDYWALKER
15. OUMACARR
16. MURDOMACCLEOD
17. DAVIDHAY
18. RAPIDVIENNA
19. SANSIRO
20. OLDTRAFFORD

Round 4 - 1990s

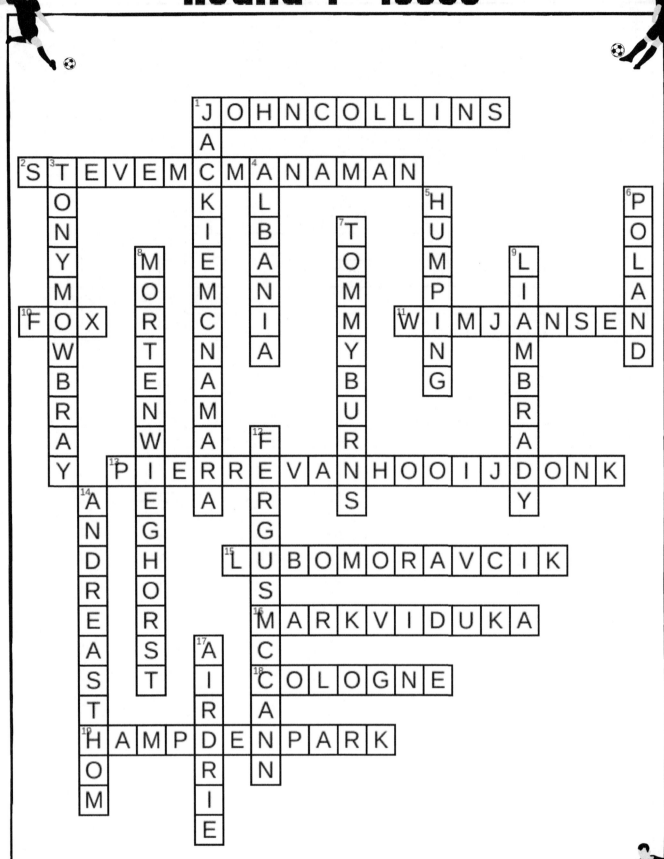

Round 5 - 2000s

1. ROYKEANE
2. ALANTHOMPSON
3. BOAVISTA
4. SCOTTMCDONALD
5. DUNDEEUNITED
6. MARTINONEILL
7. MAGNUSHEDMAN
8. CHRISSUTTON
9. BARRYROBSON
10. STEPHENMCMANUS
11. ARTURBORUC
12. JOSEMOURINHO
13. SHUNSUKENAKAMURA
14. CHRISKILLEN
15. HENRIKLARSSON
16. JOHNHARTSON
17. AIDENMCGEADY
18. BENFICA
19. LOUISSAHA
20. LIVERPOOL

Round 6 - 2010s

Across and down crossword answers:

- RONNYDEILA
- HIBERNIAN
- TONYWATT
- HEARTOFMIDLOTHIAN
- GARYHOOPER
- FREDDIELJUNGBERG
- STUARTARMSTRONG
- PADDYMCCOURT
- SPARTAKMOSCOW
- MOUSSADEMBELE
- JOHNGUIDETTI
- TOMROGIC
- GEORGIOSSAMARAS
- NEWCASTLEUNITED
- WESTBROMWICHALBION
- ROBBIEKEANE
- MIKAELLUSTIG
- KENYA
- BRENDANRODGERS
- KRISCOMMONS

2. DEMENTIA
4. ZURICH
1. YUGOSLAVIA
5. JIM CRAIG
3. ANTE
7. THIRTY
8. CATENACCIO
9. STEVIE CHALMERS
6. MANCHESTER CITY
10. RENATO CAPPELLINI
11. CZECHOSLOVAKIA
12. SEAN FALLON
13. ESTADIO NACIONAL
14. GIACINTO FACCHETTI
15. BILLY
15. BOBBY LENNOX
16. DUNDEE
17. RONNIE SIMPSON
15. SHANKLY
18. BERTIE AUD
19. BOBBY MURDOCH

Round 8 - Jock Stein

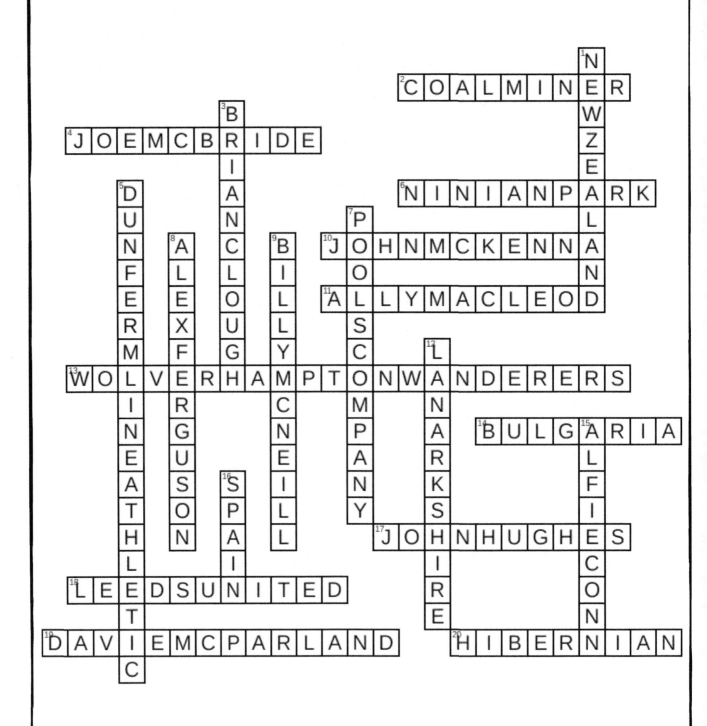

Across

2. COAL MINER
4. JOE MCBRIDE
6. NINIAN PARK
10. JOHN MCKENNA
11. ALLY MACLEOD
13. WOLVERHAMPTON WANDERERS
14. BULGARIA
17. JOHN HUGHES
18. LEEDS UNITED
19. DAVIE MCPARLAND
20. HIBERNIAN

Down

1. NEW ZEALAND
3. BRIAN CLOUGH
5. DUNFERMLINE ATHLETIC
7. POLSC COMPANY
8. ALEX FERGUSON
9. BILLY MCNEILL
12. LANARKSHIRE
15. ALFIE CONN
16. SPAIN

Round 9 - Managers

1 LIAMBRADY

3 WIMJANSEN

4 BILLYSTARK

6 LEICESTERCITY

7 EDDIEHOWE

9 ANGEPOSTECOGLOU

12 GORDONSTRACHAN

13 CHIEFSCOUT

15 NEILLENNON

16 MIDDLESBROUGH

17 WILLIEMALEY

18 NORWEGIAN

19 JOHNBARNES

Down answers (letter columns):
- **2** DAVIDHAY
- **5** JOZEFVENGLOS
- **8** JOHNKENNEDY
- **10** JIMMYMCGRORY
- **11** PAOLODICANIO
- **14** TOMMYBURNS
- **4 down** BRENANRODGER

JOHNTHOMPSON

HUGHIEGALLACHER

IRELAND

JOHNMCPHAIL

FULHAM

FIRHILL

JIMMYMCSTAY

KILMARNOCK

WILLIE

ARSENA

JOCKSTEIN

GARNGAD

HEARTOFMIDLOTHIAN

HUMENTORPEDO

ULSTER

CLYDEBANK

BOBBYLENNOX

TOMWHITE

MOTHERWELL

Round 11 - Billy McNeill

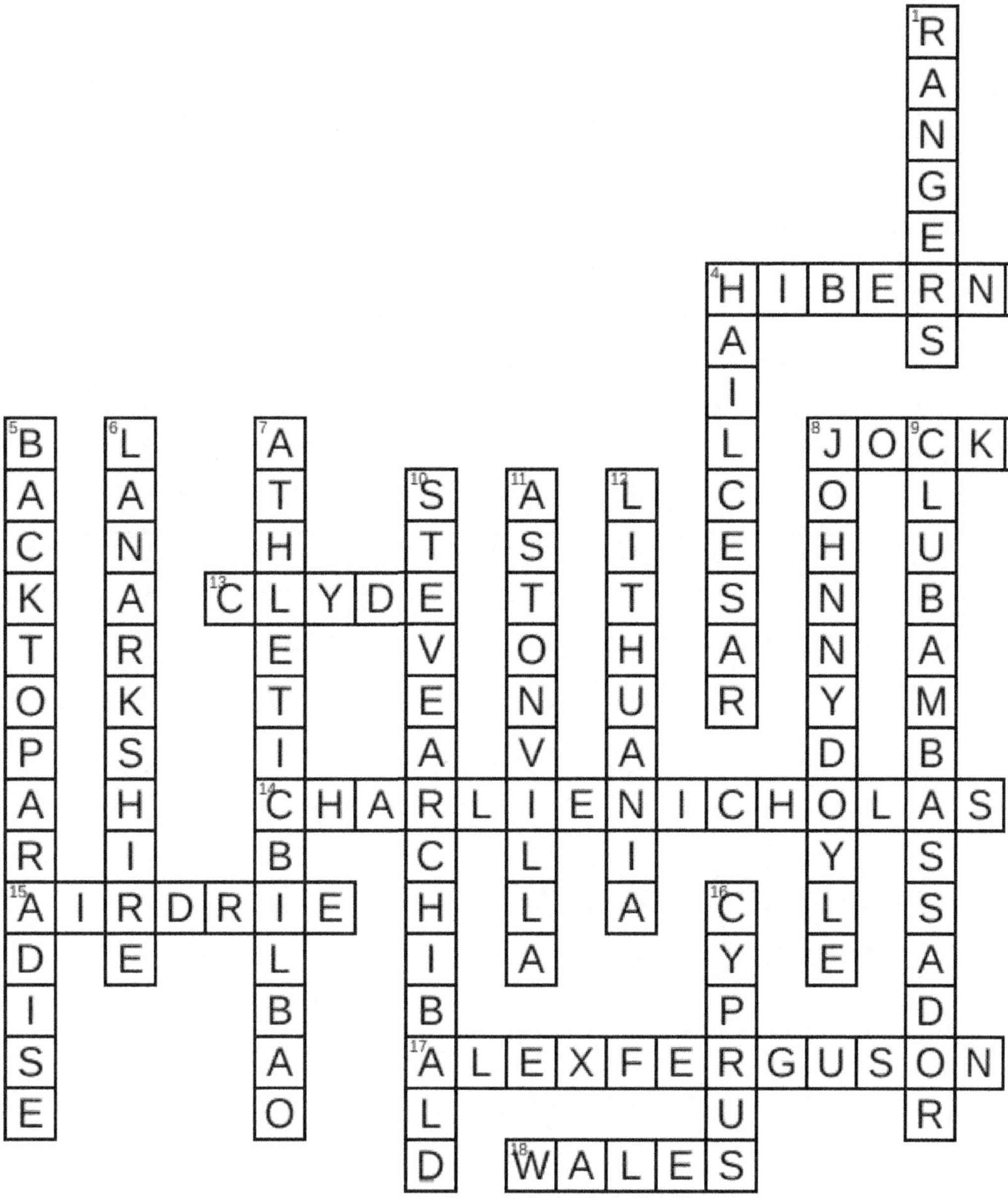

1 RANGERS
2 MANCHESTERCITY
3 DESMONDWHITE
4 HIBERNIAN
HAILCESAR
5 BACKTOPARADISE
6 LANARKSHIRE
7 ATHLETICBILBAO
8 JOCKSTEIN
JOHNNYDOYLE
9 CLUBAMBASSADOR
10 STEVEARCHIBALD
11 ASTONVILLA
12 LITHUANIA
13 CLYDE
14 CHARLIENICHOLAS
15 AIRDRIE
16 CYPRUS
17 ALEXFERGUSON
18 WALES

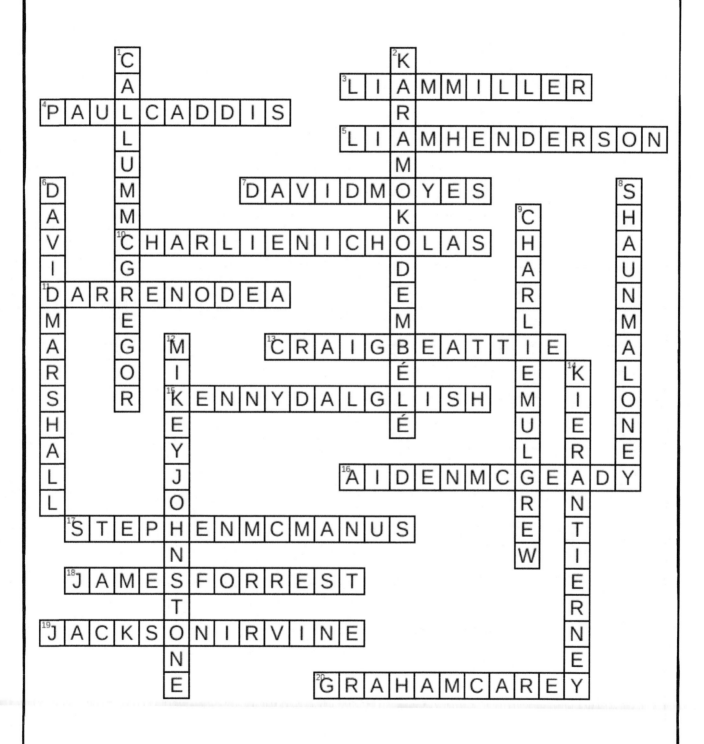

Across:

3. LIAM MILLER
4. PAUL CADDIS
5. LIAM HENDERSON
7. DAVID MOYES
10. CHARLIE NICHOLAS
11. DARREN O'DEA
13. CRAIG BEATTIE
15. KENNY DALGLISH
16. AIDEN MCGEADY
17. STEPHEN MCMANUS
18. JAMES FORREST
19. JACKSON IRVINE
20. GRAHAM CAREY

Down:

1. CALLUM MCGREGOR
2. KARAMOKO DEMBÉLÉ
6. DAVID MARSHALL
8. SHAUN MALONE
9. CHARLIE MULGREW
12. MIKEY JOHNSTONE
14. KIERAN TIERNEY

Round 14 - Club Captains

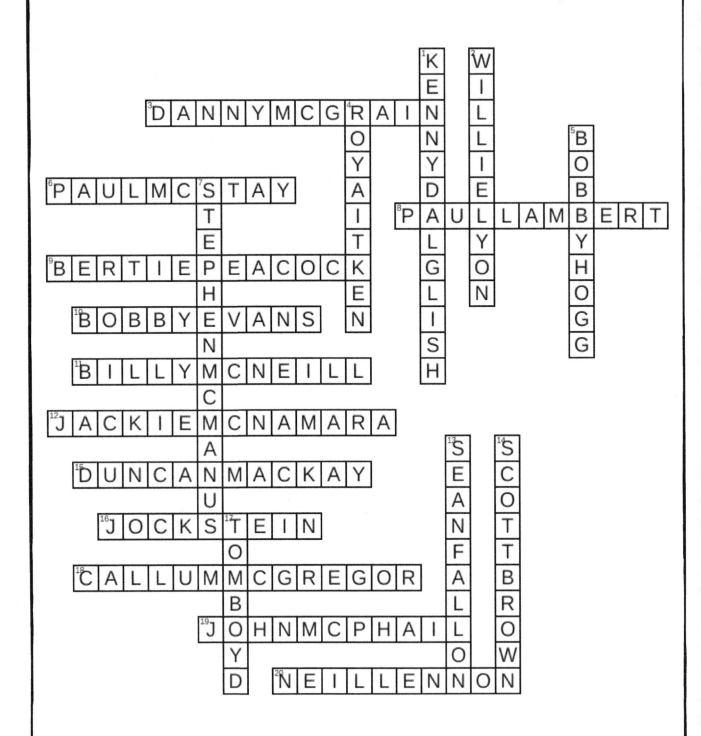

Round 15 - Henrik Larsson

2 across: UNITEDSTATES

4 across: DUNDEEUNITED

6 across: FEYENOORD

8 across: FLOORBALL

9 across: STJOHNSTONE

11 across: JUVENTUS

13 across: DUNFERMLINEATHLETICA

18 across: MANCHESTERUNITED

19 across: BARCELONA

20 across: ENGLAND

1 down: CAPEVERDE

3 down: THEKINGOFKINGS

5 down: ZLATANIBRAHIMOVIC

7 down: BENFICA

10 down: NIGERIA

12 down: HELSINGBORGS

14 down: STEFANKLOS

15 down: PAVLNEDVED

16 down: EASTERROAD

17 down: WIMJANSEN

Round 16 - Neil Lennon

1 BOLTONWANDERERS

1(down) BARCELONA

2 HIBERNIAN

3 TONYMOWBRAY

3(down) TRANMERERODVERS

4 EYALBERKOVIC

5 EMILIANOIZIZ

6 MARTINONEILL

7 ROSSCOUNTY

8 BOLTONWANDERERS

9 ROMANCATHOLIC

10 LAGUIRR

11 PAULLAMBERT

12 CREWEALEXANDRA

12(down) CRS

13 DUBAI

14 ARMAGH

15 JOELEDLEY

16 JOHANMJALLBY

17 LEICESTERCITY

18 ARTURBORUC

Across
3. MARKVIDUKA
5. CRAIGBURLEY
7. FIFTEEN
9. MASSIMODONATI
10. CENTRALCOASTMARINERS
12. BORUSSIADORTMUND
16. STILIYANPETROV
17. BRAZIL
18. UMBRO
19. DIDIERAGATHE

Down
1. JIRIJAROSIK
2. DMITRIKHARIN
4. JUNINHOPAULISTA
6. BRAMKAYAL
8. TWENTYSEVEN
11. SCOTTBROWN
13. JULIEN
14. DIONDUBLIN
15. GARYHOOPER

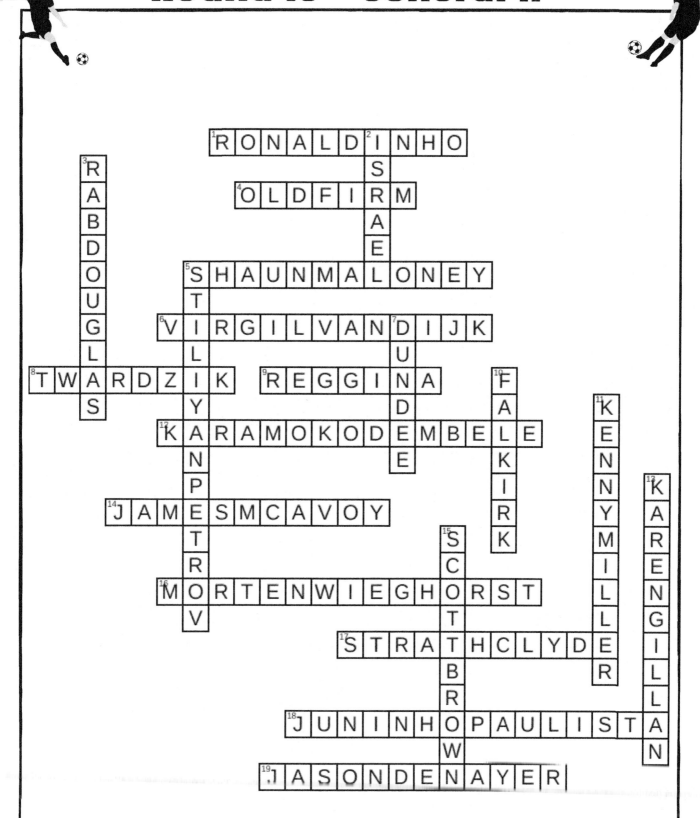

Round 19 – General II

1 RONALDINHO
2 ISRAEL
3 RABDOUGLAS
4 OLDFIRM
5 STILIYANPETROV
6 VIRGILVANDIJK
7 DUNDEE
8 TWARDZIK
9 REGGINA
10 FALKIRK
11 KENNYMILLER
12 KARAMOKODEMBELE
13 KARENGILLAN
14 JAMESMCAVOY
15 SCOTTBROW
16 MORTENWIEGHORST
17 STRATHCLYDE
18 JUNINHOPAULISTA
19 JASONDENAYER

That's all folks, thank you so much for purchasing this Celtic crossword book. I really hope you enjoyed it and learnt some cool facts about the club to impress your fellow Celts.

As a small independent publisher any reviews you can leave will be a big help as I try to grow my company and produce better and better books for you to enjoy.

If you have any criticisms, please do email me before leaving a negative review and I'd be happy to assist you if you have any problems!

kieran.brown2402@gmail.com

Printed in Great Britain
by Amazon